Anny and her husband,
1939

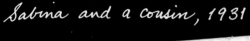

Sabina and
a friend,
1932

Sabina and a cousin, 1931

Emmy,
Yom Kippur,
1938

Sabina, age 18

Anny, Emmy, and Sabina,
ages 3, 4, and 6

Anny in front
of her home, 1936

Sabina
and
Jacob's
wedding,
Rome,
1934

Emmy, 193

GLOSSARY OF WORDS NOT DEFINED IN THE STORY

Bubi (Yiddish)—Grandmother.
challah (Yiddish)—a braided bread made with eggs,
                            traditionally made for the Sabbath.
Jüdin (German)—Jewess; female Jewish person.
Tante (German)—Aunt.
Zayde (Yiddish)—Grandfather.

For my daughter and my sons, my nieces and my nephews,
and my first grandniece, Delphine

Atheneum Books for Young Readers
An imprint of Simon & Schuster Children's Publishing Division
1230 Avenue of the Americas, New York, New York 10020
Copyright © 2005 by Marisabina Russo
Book design by Ann Bobco
The text for this book is set in Golden Cockerel.
The illustrations for this book are rendered in gouache.
Manufactured in China
First Edition
2 4 6 8 10 9 7 5 3 1
Library of Congress Cataloging-in-Publication Data
Russo, Marisabina.
Always remember me : how one family survived World War II / Marisabina Russo.— 1st ed.
p. cm.
"An Anne Schwartz Book".
ISBN 0-689-86920-7
1. Jews—Germany—Biography—Juvenile literture. 2. Jews—Persecutions—Germany—Juvenile literature.
3. Holocaust, Jewish (1939-1945)—Germany—Juvenile literature. 4. Germany—Ethnic relations—Juvenile literature.
I. Title.
DS135.G5A15865 2005
940.53'18'092—dc22
2004004228

Always Remember Me

HOW ONE FAMILY
SURVIVED
WORLD WAR II

by marisabina russo

AN ANNE SCHWARTZ BOOK • Atheneum Books for Young Readers

New York • London • Toronto • Sydney

Sunday is the most important day of the week in my family, the day we gather for dinner at my Oma's. First there are hugs and hellos. Oma is so happy to see us. She always wears her favorite dress and a gold heart hanging from a chain around her neck.

Before we eat, Oma raises her glass. "Today we celebrate!" she says. To her, every Sunday is a celebration, even when it isn't anyone's birthday. "I think I am the luckiest grandmother in the world."

When all the soup and chicken and challah have been eaten and all the plates and glasses have been cleared, Oma always lets me take out her two photo albums. One is old and worn, the pages brittle.

"This album is about my first life before I came to America," says Oma.

The other is new and clean, and inside there are even a few pictures of me.

"This album is about my second life here," she says. "Why am I so lucky to have two lives? That is a long and interesting story."

"Tell it to me, please?" I always beg as I open the first album.

"Of course," says Oma, and she begins.

"I was once a beautiful girl. See me here in my best lace dress? This was in a little town in Poland where I grew up. But my family decided to move to Germany because they'd heard Jewish people were treated better there. Less discrimination. More opportunities. Only my grandparents stayed behind—they were too old to make such a big change. Before we left, my grandmother gave me a necklace with a gold heart. 'When you wear this, always remember me,' she said, 'and may luck follow you wherever you go.'"

"It's the same necklace you're wearing now," I say.

"Yes, Rachel, you are right," says Oma, touching the heart.

We look at the next picture.

"My parents wanted me to marry the son of a rabbi, but I fell in love with your grandpa Leo. He was a traveling salesman—very dashing with his waxed mustache and gold watch. Leo and I married and moved to an apartment on a street paved with cobblestones right around the corner from the zoo. At night we could hear the lions roar!

"Our first baby was a little girl with round pink cheeks and brown eyes whom we named Sabina. She looked a lot like you."

"That's because she became my mama," I say.

"You are right," says Oma. "Every afternoon Sabina's nurse put her in a carriage and wheeled her to the zoo. Sabina learned German baby words like *Löwe,* which means 'lion,' and *Elefant,* which means 'elephant.' She liked the sea lions best of all.

"Our little family was very happy until World War One broke

out and Leo had to join the German army. I gave him my gold

heart to keep in his pocket until he was home again. 'May luck

follow you wherever you go,' I called as his train left the station.

"Leo sent me postcards and came home for short visits. During the war we had two more babies."

"Aunt Emmi and Aunt Anni," I say. I can hear them talking in the kitchen as they wash Oma's dishes.

"You are right," says Oma. "And when the war was finally over and Leo came home, we were a big, happy family in our apartment around the corner from the zoo. I put my gold heart back around my neck.

"I dressed my three little girls in matching dresses so we could have this nice picture taken in the photographer's studio. Oh, it was hard to get them to be still!

"My darling daughters! One, two, three, they followed me everywhere—to the zoo, to the park, and on Saturdays to visit their grandparents, Bubi and Zayde."

"Just the way I visit you on Sundays," I say.

"You are right," says Oma.

"Soon Sabina started school. On her first day she wore a new dress and carried a satchel with her sandwich. You see the big cone she is holding so carefully? It is called a *Zuckertüte* and was filled with candy. Sabina didn't want her sisters to touch it. She felt very grown up. 'You two babies can do your boring baby things, like visit the zoo, while I go to school,' she told them. But it wasn't long before Emmi and Anni were schoolgirls too.

"Then my Leo died suddenly. I thought my gold heart had not brought me the luck my grandmother had promised. I stopped wearing it. But Bubi said to me, 'You are still very lucky to have your daughters,' and she was right. I put my necklace back on.

"Everyone tried to help—Bubi and Zayde, Tante Sali, Uncle Oskar, Uncle Izzy, and Tante Malke. When I ran out of money, I had to pawn my jewelry."

"But you never pawned your gold heart," I say.

"You are right," says Oma.

"In time Sabina took a job after school, sewing for Uncle Izzy's men's haberdashery, and saved money for law school. Emmi helped Uncle Oskar with his bookkeeping in his fur shop. Every week Anni went to a sports club to give handball lessons. We got by."

Usually, when we reach this part, Oma quickly closes the first album and goes on to the second. There are a few pages she never wants to show me, no matter how many times I ask. But today is different.

"I think you are old enough to hear the rest of the story now," she says, and pulls me closer.

Her voice is quiet as she goes on. "This part is difficult to tell. Our lives began to change. The Nazis came into power. They made speeches everywhere against the Jews.

"When Sabina went on a school trip proudly wearing a new coat she had made, some girls refused to sit near her because she was Jewish. '*Jüdin*,' they whispered, as if it were a bad word.

"The baker would not deliver rolls to our apartment. 'I do not sell to Jews anymore,' he told me.

"Emmi's teacher made her stand in the hall while the class saluted the flag. 'After all, you are a Jew, not a German,' she said to Emmi.

"Anni could no longer go to her sports club."

"That wasn't fair," I say.

"Yes, Rachel, you are right," says Oma.

"Every day there were new laws: No Jews in the cafés. No Jews in the park. No Jews at the zoo.

"Sabina could not go to law school even though she had the highest grades in her class.

"Her boyfriend, Jacob, could not go to medical school.

"It was like a bad dream.

"One day Sabina and Jacob decided to move to Italy, where they could finish school. It broke my heart to see my first-born daughter leave our apartment around the corner from the zoo."

"It doesn't sound like you were so lucky anymore," I say.

"You are right, but part of luck is hope, and I still had lots of hope," says Oma. "Even when things got worse.

"Imagine, all of us—every Jew in Germany—had to get an identity card from the Nazi government with our picture and fingerprints and a giant red *J* as if we were criminals who couldn't be trusted.

"And then came *Kristallnacht,* the Night of Broken Glass. It started with riots in the streets. Emmi and Anni and I, we hid in our darkened apartment.

"The next day Uncle Marcus came with the terrible news: Uncle Izzy's haberdashery and Uncle Oskar's fur shop had been smashed with rocks and bottles like all the other Jewish stores in the city. Even our synagogue had been burned to the ground. I saved this newspaper clipping about that terrible night."

I close my eyes and try to imagine the stores in my neighborhood with broken windows and glass all over the sidewalk. Oma covers my hand with hers and continues.

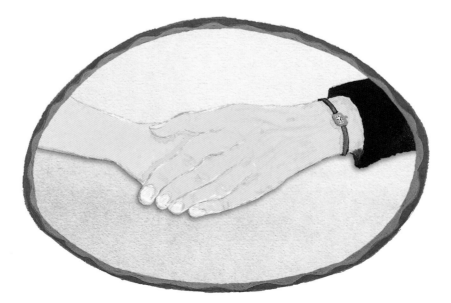

Nr. 314. Seite 5

Stadtblatt der LTZ.

Volkszorn fordert Sühne von Juda

Spontane Protestkundgebungen in Leipzig / Die Synagogen in Flammen

"I said to Emmi and Anni, 'My darlings, we are not safe here. We must leave.' They did not want to move from the place that had always been their home, but they knew we must. In the last few months they gathered lots of pictures so they would always remember. . . .

"But leaving Germany was not so easy. I wrote to my cousins, already in America. I waited in long lines in crowded offices to get all the papers we needed. Papers, so many papers! I even had to pay the government to let us go.

"Many Jews who tried to leave were not so lucky.

"My family was scattering to other countries around the world, to wherever they could go: Australia, England, Argentina, even China! I taped this small map of the world in my album and marked the places. *Someday*, I thought, *I will take a trip around the world to see my family again.*"

"Did you ever go?" I ask.

"No, Rachel, and now I am too old. But maybe someday you will." She looks at me with hope and also a little sadness.

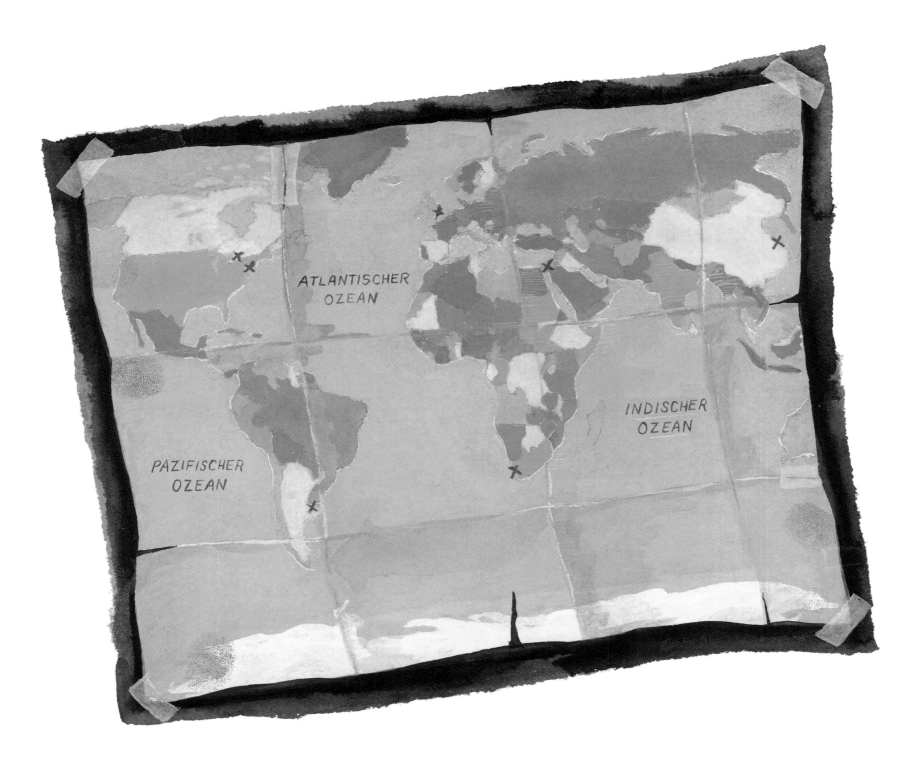

"A week before we were supposed to sail, Anni made a shocking announcement. Her boyfriend, Heinz, wanted her to stay and get married. He had no papers to go to America like we did. What could I do? I did not want to leave until all my daughters were safely out of Germany.

"And so Emmi sailed by herself. I gave her two precious things to carry for me: my photo album and my gold heart.

"'When you wear this necklace, remember me,' I told her. 'May luck follow you wherever you go.'"

HAMBURG-AMERIKA LINIE
(Compañia Hamburguesa-Americana)

No. 3657

TouristenKlasse
Clase Turista
Tourist Class

Motorschiff
motonave } Hansa
motor vessel

am
de salir } 4. Juli 1939
smiling

von
de } Hamburg
from

nach
á } New York
to

Name des Reisenden
nombre del pasajero
passenger's name

Fraulein
Emmi Neumann

Bezahlter Fahrpreis
Pasaje pagada - Farepaid

RM 500.-

5.-
3.75
RM 508.75

We have come to the end of the first album. There is a small envelope taped to the back cover. Oma opens it and pulls out a star made of cloth with the word "Jude" printed across the middle.

"And then I was all alone in the apartment around the corner from the zoo," she says quietly. "I had to start wearing this yellow star sewn to the front of my coat."

"Why?" I ask.

"Because the Nazis wanted to keep track of us, make sure we didn't go places where Jews were not allowed. They took all my jewelry. It was lucky I had given the gold heart to Emmi.

"A year went by. My daughters had all gotten married and I had only been able to go to Anni's wedding." Oma points to two pictures that sit in frames on a nearby table. "These are all I saw of your mama's and Emmi's weddings.

"One morning I heard loud knocking on my door. There was a policeman holding a sheet of paper with my name on it. He said it was time for me to go to a concentration camp."

Oma stops talking. She looks at me with faraway eyes, and for a moment I think she has made a mistake. This can't be a story about being lucky. I know that a concentration camp was a place where Jewish people were hurt and often killed.

Oma closes the album now and goes on.

"There was a war that spread from country to country all around the world until it was called World War Two. Somehow I survived the dismal years in the concentration camp until the war was over. How? Maybe it was because I was determined to see my daughters again. Maybe it was because I was lucky, though I didn't feel that way. I had been starved and cold and had seen people shot for no reason except that they were Jewish. I had slept on hard bunks and worn dirty clothing. I had no idea where my beautiful daughters were.

"At last the war ended, and the American soldiers sent me home. Our building was gone, just a pile of rubble from all the bombs. You could stand where our front door had been and see all the way to the gates of the zoo."

I shut my eyes and can't help but see the pictures in my head of all that Oma is telling me.

"I stayed in a building nearby with people like me who had no homes. And then, a miracle! Anni found me. Oh, how thin she was! She had survived the concentration camp in Poland called Auschwitz and a death march through the snow. Her husband was dead."

"What was the death march?" I whisper.

Oma squeezes my hand. "When the Nazis saw they were losing, they began to retreat to Germany, and they forced the prisoners to go too—to walk away from Auschwitz. Anyone who was weak or who stumbled was shot. Anni had gotten no food, only snow to drink. But she'd managed to escape and hide in a barn.

"And then, more miracles! Anni wrote a letter to Emmi and gave it to an American soldier who was going home. Emmi answered with news of Sabina; Jacob had been killed and she had been shot in the knee. But she had hidden in the mountains of Italy and survived. I cried with joy. My daughters were alive! Maybe luck had managed to follow me after all."

Oma looks as if she might cry. I feel my tears coming too, so I squeeze her hand and ask her to get to the happy part, the part in the new album. I open it, and there are the pictures of my mother, Aunt Emmi, and Aunt Anni, the way they looked a year after the war was over. Below, Oma had written:

My Three Beautiful Daughters

"First Anni, then Sabina, and finally me, we all came to this country. We didn't have much to bring with us: my yellow star, Anni's blue numbers tattooed on her arm by the guards at Auschwitz, Sabina's scar from the bullet. It didn't matter. We were a family again. When I saw Emmi at the pier, she was wearing my gold heart. She said she had worn it every day and night of the war."

"A few years later your mama, Sabina, married your father." Oma smiles and strokes my cheek with her hand. "And now I am here in America," she says, "with a beautiful granddaughter. Of course I am the luckiest Oma in the world."

I turn the page and there is a picture of a tiny girl sitting on the floor with a bow in her hair and a small leather satchel over her shoulder. Oma, Mama, Aunt Emmi, and Aunt Anni are all in a row behind her, smiling.

The little girl is me.

There are many empty pages in the back of the second album. Oma says they will be my pages to fill with pictures.

"One day you can tell your own grandchild about how your family's love gave them the strength to survive their darkest days," says Oma.

Now that we are at the end of Oma's story I start to put her albums away, but she tells me to wait. "It is time for the necklace from my grandmother in Poland to go to my granddaughter in America," she says.

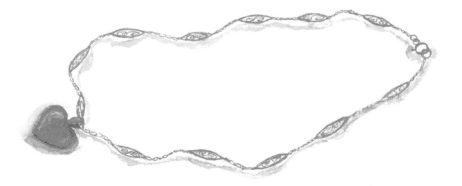

She reaches behind her neck to open the clasp, then fastens the chain around my neck. I touch the gold heart. It feels smooth and cool.

"When you wear this necklace," says Oma, "always remember me and the story of my two lives. May luck follow you wherever you go."

AFTERWORD

My grandmother raised my mother and my two aunts in Germany in the 1920s when Jewish people could still live like their neighbors. My family never planned to leave Germany. It was their home.

In 1933 Adolf Hitler was appointed Chancellor of Germany. He used his power to get rid of all the other political parties so that no one could challenge him, organized bonfires to burn books he did not approve of, and began to stir up anti-Semitism—hatred toward Jews—with speeches and new laws.

At first German Jews thought that such a leader would never last, his ideas were so crazy. But over the following years Hitler built a strong army and police force. More people began to support him, while others were afraid to challenge him. In 1935 he passed the first of his many Nuremberg Laws, one that said that Jews were no longer citizens of Germany. And so he took away Jews' rights.

In the 1930s the Nazis (the name for Hitler and his followers, which comes from the name of their political party—the National Socialists) had created prisons, called "concentration camps," for people who opposed their government. After *Kristallnacht* (the Night of Broken Glass) they began to send Jews to these camps in great numbers. Upon arrival many prisoners were killed in gas chambers, while some of the "luckier" ones were allowed to live in crowded barracks with little food or water but were still expected to work from morning to night.

Hitler was not satisfied with his power in Germany. Within days of the German invasion of Poland in 1939, France and Great Britain declared war on Germany, and World War II began. It was a long and destructive war, involving more and more countries each year.

In 1945 Germany and its allies were defeated by the United States, Great Britain, and the Soviet Union, and the surviving prisoners of the concentration camps were freed. But more than six million Jews throughout Europe had been killed, along with many people of other faiths. This period in European history is now often called the "Holocaust," the time of a huge, tragic loss of life.

Miraculously my grandmother, my mother, and my two aunts—four Jewish women of one family—managed to survive the Holocaust, each in her own way. Their stories are the ones I heard as a child while sitting at the dinner table on Sunday afternoons. I thought that they were the bravest women in the world and that I was very lucky to be their granddaughter, daughter, and niece. I still do. It is the reason I wrote this book.

Oma,
Poland,
1904

Anny (second from left) and Emmy (third from right)
with classmates, 1922

Sabina, age 19

Emmy with Zuckertüte,
1921

Sabina and
Emmy
with nurse,
1917

Jacob, 1932

Sabina,
1921

Sabina
at the Zoo,
1915